P9-CAB-969

Technology That Changed the World

The Computer

Passport to the Digital Age

Joanne Mattern

The Rosen Publishing Group's
PowerKids Press™
New York

Published in 2003 by The Rosen Publishing Group, Inc.
29 East 21st Street, New York, NY 10010

First Edition

Book Design: Michael DeLisio and Sam Jordan

Photo Credits: Cover © R.W. Jones/Corbis; pp. 4, 5 © Archivo Iconografico, S.A./Corbis; p. 7 © Culver Pictures; pp. 8, 9, 10, 11 © Bettmann/Corbis; p. 13 © Tim O'Hara/Corbis; p. 14 © Photodisc; p. 15 © Ron Watts/Corbis; p. 16 © Liu Liquin/Corbis; p. 17 © Terry Vine/Corbis; p.18 © FPG International/Getty Images; p. 19 © Corbis; p. 20 © John Wilkes Studio/Corbis; p. 21 © Owen Franken/Corbis

Library of Congress Cataloging-in-Publication Data

Mattern, Joanne, 1963–
The computer : passport to the digital age / Joanne Mattern.
   p. cm. — (Technology that changed the world)
Summary: Presents information on computers, from the abacus to the laptop, including their invention, history, how modern-day computers work, and how they have affected people's lives.
Includes bibliographical references and index.
ISBN 0-8239-6492-2 (library binding)
1. Electronic digital computers—Juvenile literature. [1. Computers—History.] I. Title.
QA76.52 .M38 2003
004'.09—dc21
                                        2002000509

Contents

Smart Machines

People have been making and using number-counting tools for thousands of years. However, in the 1600s, the first automatic calculators were made. In 1623, Wilhelm Schikard invented a machine that could add numbers.

Blaise Pascal

In 1642, Blaise Pascal invented a machine that could add *and* subtract numbers.

In the early 1670s, Gottfried Wilhelm Leibniz added more wheels to Pascal's machine so that it could also multiply and divide numbers. These early calculators led to the invention of the modern computer.

Pascal used wheels on his machine to add and subtract numbers.

In 1801, Joseph-Marie Jacquard made a kind of computer to help him make cloth. It was called the Jacquard loom. The loom used cards, called punch cards, that had patterns of holes in them. The punch cards told the loom to make different patterns in cloth.

Now You Know

When Jacquard died in 1834, 30,000 of his looms had been made and were being used in France. Today, the Jacquard loom is still used to make cloth for furniture.

Some people who made cloth by hand were angry that Jacquard invented his loom. These people thought the loom would do their work and they would lose their jobs. Jacquard thought the angry people would hurt him so he left his hometown.

Charles Babbage spent about 40 years working on his ideas for computers. In the 1830s, he planned a machine that could do math, save information, and print. Babbage never finished building his machine, but his ideas would be used about 100 years later in making computers.

Herman Hollerith invented a machine that was used for the 1890 U.S. census. Fifty-six of Hollerith's machines took just one day to count and record information about six million people.

Charles Babbage called his early computer the Difference Engine.

The First Computers

In the 1900s, computer technology got better. In 1944, Howard Aiken built the Mark I calculating computer. It could add two numbers in less than a second and do multiplications in three seconds.

Mauchly and ENIAC

ENIAC was huge. It weighed more than 60,000 pounds. It filled a 50-by-30-foot basement room at the University of Pennsylvania in Philadelphia. Part of this machine can be seen today at the Smithsonian Institution in Washington, D.C.

In 1945, J. Presper Eckert, Jr. and John William Mauchly built a computer called ENIAC. It ran about 1,000 times faster than the Mark I. It could do about 5,000 additions and 1,000 multiplications per second. It was used by the United States government.

UNIVAC being used to count the 1954 U.S. census

In 1951, Eckert and Mauchly improved ENIAC by making the UNIVAC computer. UNIVAC was the first computer to read both number and letter characters. It was also the first computer to be used by businesses.

How Computers Work

To work, computers must be told what to do by people. The orders that people give to a computer are called programs. Computer programs let people use computers to do math, write letters, play video games, and much more.

Monitor

Computer

Keyboard

Mouse

The computer, the monitor, the keyboard, and the mouse are called hardware. Programs, video games, and anything else that tells a computer what to do are called software.

In 1959, the computer chip was invented. Computer chips carry out the orders in the computer programs and save information that helps run the computer. These chips led to the invention of the home, or personal, computer.

Some computer chips are about the size of a person's fingernail.

In later years, computers became smaller, faster, and smarter. They could solve more problems. Computers also became cheaper to make and easier for people to use. Today's small computers, called laptops, are more powerful than the huge computers built in the 1950s.

The Internet

The Internet is a system that lets computers all around the world send information to one another. People use the Internet to send messages, find answers to questions, listen to music, and much more.

The Internet has made it possible for people to run worldwide businesses from their homes.

People can go to stores where they can use computers to get on the Internet.

Computers in Business and at Home

Early computers were made to do only math. Today, computers are used in almost every part of life. The book you are reading was made using computers. Computers also help make the cars we drive and the clothes we wear.

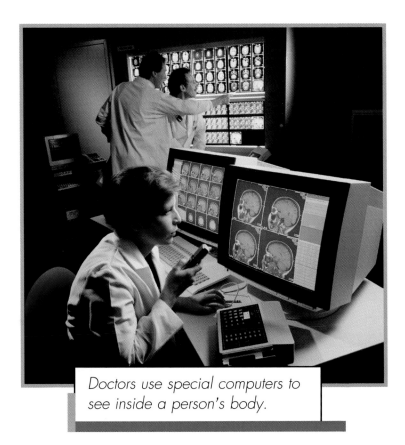

Doctors use special computers to see inside a person's body.

Scientists use computers to help
run the space shuttle and satellites.

Computers give us information about almost anything we want in just minutes, or even seconds. Computers also let us share our ideas with people all over the world faster and easier than ever before. Computers have changed the way we live.

Most laptop computers weigh about six pounds. The Mark I computer was more than 50 feet long, weighed 5 tons, and had more than 750,000 parts.

There are over 625 million computers in use all over the world today. This includes computers made for businesses, schools, and the home.

Time Line

1623: Schikard invents a machine that can add.

1642: Pascal invents a machine that can add and subtract.

1671: Leibniz makes a machine that can multiply and divide.

1801: Jacquard invents the Jacquard loom.

1830s: Babbage plans a machine that can save information.

1890: Hollerith invents a machine to count the U.S. census.

1944: Aiken builds the Mark I computer.

1945: Eckert and Mauchly build the ENIAC computer.

1951: Eckert and Mauchly build the UNIVAC computer.

1959: The computer chip is invented.

1990s: Millions of people all over the world use the Internet.

Glossary

automatic (aw-tuh-**mat**-ihk) moving or acting by itself

calculators (**kal**-kyuh-lay-tuhrz) machines that figure out math problems

census (**sehn**-suhs) a count of all the people living in a country

computer (kuhm-**pyoo**-tuhr) a machine that can store and get back knowledge, and quickly work out hard problems

hardware (**hahrd**-wair) the computer and any machine used with it, such as the keyboard, the monitor, and the mouse

loom (**loom**) a machine used for making cloth

patterns (**pat**-uhrnz) the way colors and shapes appear over and over again on cloth

personal (**per**-suh-nuhl) having to do with one person

programs (**proh**-gramz) orders for a computer that tell it what to do

scientists (**sy**-uhn-tihsts) people who study the world by using tests and experiments

software (**sawft**-wair) programs for a computer

solve (**sahlv**) to find the answer to a problem

technology (tehk-**nahl**-uh-jee) to use knowledge and science to make an easier way of doing something

Resources

Books

Why Doesn't My Floppy Disk Flop?
by Peter Cook and Scott Manning
John Wiley & Sons (1999)

Computers All Around Us
by Jim Drake
Heinemann Library (1999)

Web Sites

Due to the changing nature of Internet links, PowerKids Press has developed an online list of Web sites related to the subjects of this book. This site is updated regularly. Please use this link to access the list:

http://www.powerkidslinks.com/tcw/comp/

Index

Word Count: 469

Note to Librarians, Teachers, and Parents

If reading is a challenge, Reading Power is a solution! Reading Power is perfect for readers who want high-interest subject matter at an accessible reading level. These fact-filled, photo-illustrated books are designed for readers who want straightforward vocabulary, engaging topics, and a manageable reading experience. With clear picture/text correspondence, leveled Reading Power books put the reader in charge. Now readers have the power to get the information they want and the skills they need in a user-friendly format.